A GIFT
for
CHRISTMAS

A GIFT
for
CHRISTMAS

Michael O'Mara Books Limited

First published in Great Britain
in 2009 by
Michael O'Mara Books Limited
9 Lion Yard
Tremadoc Road
London SW4 7NQ

A CIP catalogue record for this book
is available from the British Library.

ISBN 978-1-84317-408-0

1 2 3 4 5 6 7 8 9 10

www.mombooks.com

Printed and bound in China
by WKT

'I will honour Christmas in my heart, and try to keep it all the year.'

CHARLES DICKENS

THE MEANING OF CHRISTMAS

The true meaning of Christmas is, of course, that it is the day on which Jesus Christ was born. From this stems every other Christmas tradition, both religious and celebratory.

❦

'And she brought forth her firstborn son, and wrapped him in swaddling clothes, and laid him in a manger; because there was no room for him in at the inn.'

FROM LUKE 2:7

❦

ADVENT

In the Christian calendar, Advent – which normally begins on the Sunday that falls closest to 30 November – refers to the four-week period before Christmas Day when Christians prepare for the forthcoming celebration of Christ's birth. The word 'advent' comes from the Latin, meaning 'coming towards'. Christmas wreathes contain four candles representing the four Sundays before Christmas, a time that the Christian church used to observe very seriously, banishing all marriages during it and encouraging fasting.

Advent calendars are a relatively recent addition to the Christmas tradition – starting in

the nineteenth century among
Protestant families in Germany.
The first printed advent calendar
was made by Gerhard Lang, who
was given homemade versions
by his mother and who wanted to
share his sense of enchantment at
this most simple of gifts.

The Advent candle or
'Christmas Clock' appeared later
in the nineteenth century and
also originated in Germany. The
days leading up to Christmas are
printed horizontally down the side
of the candle, and each evening
when the candle is lit a day is
melted away until, by Christmas,
there is nothing left of the candle.

THE TWELVE DAYS OF CHRISTMAS

This popular song, which dates from the twelfth century, refers to the twelve days after Christmas – that is from Boxing Day on the 26 December to the Epiphany on 5 January. The song itself is cumulative, meaning that each verse is built upon the previous verses and the lyrics refer amusingly to the increasingly expensive and ludicrous gifts that 'my true love' gives to the singer – gifts which, by the end of the song, add up to a grand total of 364!

*On the first day of Christmas my
true love sent to me a partridge
in a pear tree.*

*On the second day of Christmas my
true love sent to me two turtle doves.*

*On the third day of Christmas
my true love sent to me three
French hens.*

*On the fourth day of Christmas
my true love sent to me four
calling birds.*

*On the fifth day of Christmas my
true love sent to me five gold rings.*

*On the sixth day of Christmas my
true love sent to me six
geese a-laying.*

*On the seventh day of Christmas
my true love sent to me seven
swans a-swimming.*

*On the eighth day of Christmas
my true love sent to me eight
maids a-milking.*

*On the ninth day of Christmas
my true love sent to me nine
ladies dancing.*

*On the tenth day of Christmas my
true love sent to me ten
lords a-leaping.*

*On the eleventh day of Christmas
my true love sent to me eleven
pipers piping.*

*On the twelfth day of Christmas
my true love sent to me twelve
drummers drumming.*

WHO IS
SANTA CLAUS?

Santa Claus is known throughout the world, even in countries that are not traditionally Christian. Below are just a few examples of the different names the man we know as Santa Claus or Father Christmas is given abroad.

In Greece Santa Claus is known as *Hagios Nikolaos*.

In Brazil Santa Claus is known as *Papai Noel*.

In China Santa Claus is known as *Dun Che Lao Ren*, which translates as 'Christmas Old Man'.

In the Netherlands Santa Claus is known as *Sinterklass*.

In Estonia Santa Claus is known as *Jõuluvana*.

In Croatia Santa Claus is known as *Djed Mraz*, which translates as 'Frost Grandfather'.

In Austria Santa Claus is known as *Christkind*, which translates as 'Christ child'.

In France Santa Claus is known as *Père Noël*.

In Italy Santa Claus is known as *Babbo Natale*.

CHRISTMAS PUDDING

There is no better custom than that of the Christmas pudding! Sometimes known as 'Plum Pudding' (although the recipe contains no plums), this delicious fare is traditionally made on the first Sunday of Advent. The ingredients, which include currants, sultanas, candied peel and almonds – along, usually, with a generous glass of brandy – should be stirred from east to west, to remind us of the journey the Three Wise Men made to Bethlehem, and each member of the family is supposed to take a turn stirring everything up.

Sometimes a sixpence (or nowadays a £1.00 coin) is

dropped in to the mixture, bestowing good luck on the person who finds it on Christmas Day (so long as it doesn't break a tooth or, worse, isn't swallowed).

'If December ice will bear a duck Thereafter will be slush and muck'
ANONYMOUS

CHRISTMAS CRACKERS

The Christmas cracker was created in the nineteenth century by Thomas Smith. Smith was a confectioner who visited Paris and was impressed by the pretty bon-bons (sugar-coated almonds) he saw there, which came wrapped in brightly coloured twists of tissue paper.

Some years later, Smith took this idea and created the first Christmas cracker in England, which sold moderately well. However, wanting to develop the cracker further, over subsequent Christmases, Smith placed little love poems inside each one and

later still he added the small explosive strip that makes the cracker go BANG!

It is believed that the largest cracker in the world – measuring 63.1 metres long and 4 metres wide – was made in 2001 by children from Ley Hill School in Buckinghamshire.

❧

'Unless we make Christmas an occasion to share our blessings, all the snow in Alaska won't make it white.'

BING CROSBY

❧

MINSTRELS – WILLIAM WORDSWORTH

*The minstrels played their
Christmas tune
To-night beneath my cottage-eaves;
While, smitten by a lofty moon,
The encircling laurels,
thick with leaves,
Gave back a rich and
dazzling sheen,
That overpowered their
natural green.*

*Through hill and valley
every breeze
Had sunk to rest with folded wings;
Keen was the air, but
could not freeze,
Nor check the music of the strings;*

So stout and hardy were the band
That scraped the chords with
strenuous hand.

And who but listened?
– till was paid
Respect to every inmate's claim,
The greeting given,
the music played,
In honour of each household name,
Duly pronounced with lusty call,
And 'Merry Christmas'
wished to all.

THE CHRISTMAS STAR

The star that led the Three Wise Men to the newborn king is one of the enduring images of Christmas and has come to symbolize good fortune, luck and happiness.

In Poland, after the Christmas Eve meal, the village priest acts the part of the 'star man' and tests the children on their religious knowledge.

In Hungary, a star-shaped pattern carved in an apple is said to bring good fortune.

In Alaska, children carry a star-shaped figure around from house to house in the hope of

receiving treats and sweets from
householders.

BOXING DAY

The celebration of Boxing Day is
almost entirely confined to English-
speaking countries and is said
to have originated in the Middle
Ages, when churches would open
their alms boxes, in which the
congregation had placed money
throughout the year. The money
would then be distributed among
the neighbourhood poor.

Nowadays, it is far more likely
that people celebrate the day
by going out shopping in
the Christmas Sales!

THE MOST POPULAR CHRISTMAS CAROL

Commonly believed to have originated in the fifteenth century, the Christmas carol was a sign of the emancipation of the people from the old Puritanism which had for so long suppressed any dance and drama, denounced communal singing and generally fought against any sign that people might want to enjoy themselves by singing up-tempo songs. In accordance with this, one of the most loved carols must be 'God Rest Ye Merry Gentlemen':

God rest ye merry gentlemen,
Let nothing you dismay;
Remember, Christ our Saviour
Was born upon this day,
To save us all from Satan's power
When we were gone astray.
O tidings of comfort and joy,
Comfort and joy,
O tidings of comfort and joy.

In Bethlehem, in Israel,
This blessed Babe was born,
And laid within a manger
Upon this blessed morn;
That which His Mother Mary
Did nothing take in scorn.
O tidings of comfort and joy,
Comfort and joy,
O tidings of comfort and joy.

WASSAILING

Sadly, these days, the tradition of 'wassailing' is not often observed, but originally it was an extremely popular pastime, which involved a lot of drinking and singing. The word itself comes from the Anglo-Saxon *'waes hael'* meaning 'good health', and strictly speaking applies to a beverage made up from a mixture of ingredients such as roasted apples, eggs, ale, nuts, spices and curdled cream.

According to several sources there is a legend attached to the tradition of 'wassailing' that involves a beautiful, young Saxon girl called Rowena, who made a gift of a bowl of wine to a handsome Prince called

Vortigen with the words *'waes hael'*. Thereafter, the tradition of wassailing involves passing the said beverage round the room in a large bowl to the accompaniment of much music and merriment, after which the wassail is duly consumed!

'There's nothing sadder in this world than to awake Christmas morning and not be a child.'

ERMA BOMBECK

THE CHRISTMAS TREE

According to the history books, it was theologian and academic Martin Luther who first introduced Christmas lights to the fir tree. Walking through a forest near his home in Wittenberg, Saxony, it is said that he gazed up at the night sky only to think of the star that led the Three Wise Men to Jesus's crib. Taking a small fir tree home, he later decorated it with candles, after which he sat his children around him and began to tell them about his walk through the forest and the story of Jesus's birth.

The decoration of Christmas trees with baubles was very popular in Germany throughout the sixteenth and seventeenth

centuries – in fact so popular
was it that when the first German
immigrants settled in Pennsylvania,
USA, they took the custom with
them.

In England, the Christmas tree
first became popular when, in
1851, Queen Victoria's husband,
Prince Albert, brought a tree
over from Germany and had it
erected at Windsor Castle. The
royal family were then illustrated
standing around the tree – a
picture that appeared in all the
newspapers of the day, after which
it became very fashionable for
everyone to adopt the tradition.

A CHRISTMAS RHYME

God bless the master of this house,
And its good mistress too,
And all the little children
That round the table go;
And all your kin and kinsmen,
That dwell both far and near;
We wish you a merry Christmas
And a happy New Year.

ANONYMOUS

'A lovely thing about Christmas
is that it's compulsory, like a
thunderstorm, and we all go
through it together.'

GARRISON KEILLOR

RUDOLPH

Everyone knows the name of Santa Claus's lead reindeer, Rudolph, the proud possessor of a very famous red nose, but the names of the other reindeer are often forgotten, so here is a little reminder.

Dasher

Dancer

Prancer

Vixen

Comet

Cupid

Donner (originally known
as Dunder or Donder)

Blitzen (originally known
as Blixem)

In fact, Rudolph wasn't in Santa's
original reindeer line-up – he only
joined when the song 'Rudolph the
Red-Nosed Reindeer' was written
about him in 1949 by Johnny
Marks. The song was first recorded
by Gene Autry.

*'The only blind person at
Christmastime is he who has
not Christmas in his heart.'*
HELEN KELLER

THE HOLLY AND THE IVY

Both these evergreens, so closely associated with Christmastime, have different symbolic meanings that go back centuries. Ivy was a symbol of eternal life in the pagan world and came to represent new promise and eternal life in the Christian tradition, while holly has come to stand for peace and joy – and people are said to settle arguments under a holly tree.

*'Christmas gift suggestions:
To your enemy, forgiveness.
To an opponent, tolerance.
To a friend, your heart.
To a customer, service.
To all, charity.
To every child, a good example.
To yourself, respect.'*

OREN ARNOLD

MISTLETOE

Of all the plants in our forests and woodlands, mistletoe (particularly that which grows on oak trees) has to be the most sacred. Considered by Celtic Druids to have magical

powers, such as promoting
fertility and warding off evil spirits,
mistletoe was in use long before
the birth of Christ, and thus
the custom of kissing under
the mistletoe to bestow good
luck for the forthcoming year
(or marriage between the two
people kissing) is more a pagan
than a Christian one.

CANDY CANES

When Christmas trees became
popular in the Victorian period,
people decided that alongside
baubles and candles, it would be
pretty to hang candy canes (as
well as other foodstuffs, such as
strings of dried fruit) on their tree.

That said, the earliest reference to the candy cane in relation to Christmas dates from 1670, when an elderly choirmaster from Cologne Cathedral allegedly decided to give all the children a piece of candy in order to keep them happy and quiet during the nativity service. According to legend, it was this same choirmaster who bent the candy cane into the shape of a shepherd's staff.

TURKEY

A relative newcomer to the traditional Christmas – turkeys weren't readily available in the United Kingdom until the 1950s and even then they weren't suitable for every family, as they were generally too large to fit in either the fridges or ovens of that period. Nowadays, however, at least ninety per cent of the country sits down to roast turkey on Christmas Day, accompanied by a wide range of vegetables and, of course, stuffing. Prior to turkey being served at Christmas, swans, geese, pheasants and the occasional boar's head were the meats most likely to appear on the yuletide table.

AN EXTRACT FROM
A VISIT FROM
ST NICHOLAS

'He was dressed all in fur from his
head to his foot,
And his clothes were all tarnished
with ashes and soot;
A bundle of toys he had flung on
his back,
And he looked like a peddler just
opening his sack.
His eyes: how they twinkled! His
dimples: how merry!
His cheeks were like roses, his nose
like a cherry;
His droll little mouth was drawn up
like a bow,
And the beard on his chin was as
white as the snow.

The stump of a pipe he held tight in his teeth,
And the smoke it encircled his head like a wreath.
He had a broad face, and a little round belly
That shook when he laughed like a bowl full of jelly.
He was chubby and plump, a right jolly old elf
And I laughed when I saw him, in spite of myself!'

CLEMENT C. MOORE, 1882

CHRISTMAS STOCKINGS

As a child, few things are as exciting as waking up on Christmas morning to feel the weight or catch a glimpse of a Christmas stocking at the end of your bed. But given that some Christmas traditions can be dated back to the Middle Ages, the custom of hanging up stockings for Santa Claus to fill with presents is thought to be relatively new.

That said, several legends are attached to the tradition, the most popular of which involves two young sisters whose father was very poor. He worried constantly about what would happen to

his girls after he died, until one Christmas Eve, Santa Claus was passing through the village and, knowing of the father's plight but not wanting to offend the old man by offering charity, he decided to give the girls a bag of gold coins each. Santa Claus came down the chimney but then had to find a good place to hide the coins – which he did – in the girls' stockings!

Not all children, however, receive treats, for tradition dictates that a child who is naughty during the year should only receive a lump of coal. Boooo hiss!

THE COLOURS OF CHRISTMAS

Traditionally, red and green are the colours of Christmas. Red symbolizes the blood Christ shed when he was crucified, while green symbolizes re-growth and the continuance of life through the cold, dark days of winter.

'Roses are reddish
Violets are bluish
If it wasn't for Christmas
We'd all be Jewish!'
BENNY HILL

SILENT NIGHT

'Silent Night' (*Stille Nacht. Helige Nacht*) is first thought to have been sung over 180 years ago by a village choir in Austria. It is one of the most popular Christmas carols, known and sung worldwide, although it was during the First World War that it was sung to most poignant effect.

On Christmas Eve 1914, British and German troops called a halt to the fighting and for a few brief hours sang carols to each other from the trenches. 'Silent Night' was one of the few songs known by both sides, and those soldiers who returned to tell the tale said it was one of the most deeply moving moments of their lives.

CHRISTMAS IS COMING

Christmas is coming,
The geese are getting fat,
Please to put a penny
In the old man's hat.

If you haven't got a penny,
A ha'penny will do;
If you haven't got a ha'penny
Then God bless you!

ANONYMOUS

What do you call a person who's afraid of Santa Claus?
Claustrophobic!

42

ADVENT WREATHES

As well as Advent calendars and Advent candles, there is also a strong tradition of Advent wreathes in most Christian countries. The wreath is round in shape – with no beginning or end, thus symbolizing eternal life – and is made up from winter evergreens such as holly and ivy, which are supposed to represent the triumph of life through the dark winter months. Traditionally four candles are placed in the wreath – one to be lit on each Sunday leading up to Christmas.

BE CAREFUL WHAT PRESENTS YOU CHOOSE!

Here is a lovely anecdote from *Braude's Handbook of Stories for Toastmasters and Speakers* about the perils of giving someone (particularly a child) the wrong gift at Christmas.

Little Georgie received a new drum for Christmas, and shortly thereafter, when father came home from work one evening, mother said: 'I don't think that man upstairs likes to hear Georgie play his drum, but he's certainly subtle about it.'

'Just what do you mean?' asked the father.

'Well,' said Georgie's mother, 'this afternoon he gave Georgie a knife and asked him if he knew what was inside the drum.'

CHRISTINGLE

The tradition of the Christingle (a lit candle that is normally set in an orange to symbolize Christ as the light of the world), was begun by the Moravian Church, but in the mid-twentieth century was also adopted by the Church of England. The word is most likely of German origin, *Christkindl* meaning 'Christ child', and the custom of lighting these candles is still usually practiced most among children.

WHITE CHRISTMAS

One of, if not *the* most enduring of all Christmas songs has to be 'White Christmas', which was composed in 1942 by the American songwriter Irving Berlin and which was famously performed by Bing Crosby (alongside co-star Marjorie Reynolds) in the film *Holiday Inn* in the same year. Now, nearly seventy years later, the song is still played, performed and enjoyed every Christmas, and is still loved all over the world.

CHRISTMAS CARDS

W.C.T. Dobson RA, is generally believed to have sent the first Christmas card in 1844, and two years later, in 1846, the first commercial Christmas card was printed, courtesy of Sir Henry Cole (director of the Victoria and Albert Museum) and J. C. Horsley.

This card however, was widely condemned by the British Temperance Society, who disapproved of the picture as it represented a family group drinking alcohol. Finally, in the 1870s, the art printers, Tucks, began mass producing Christmas cards, after which the custom of sending cards to friends and family really took the nation by storm.

THE OXEN

Thomas Hardy is one of the best loved of all English novelists. A traditional storyteller who revelled in the telling of sad tales, perhaps his most famous book is *Tess of the D'Urbervilles*. But Hardy was not only a brilliant novelist, he was also a poet of some note. Printed below is a beautiful poem describing the night of Christ's birth.

Christmas Eve, and twelve
of the clock.
'Now they are all on their knees,'
An elder said as we sat in a flock
By the embers in hearthside ease.

We pictured the meek mild
creatures where
They dwelt in their strawy pen,
Nor did it occur to one of us there
To doubt they were kneeling then.

So fair a fancy few would weave
In these years! Yet, I feel,
If someone said on Christmas Eve,
'Come; see the oxen kneel,

'In the lonely barton by
yonder coomb
Our childhood used to know,'
I should go with him in the gloom,
Hoping it might be so.

TWELFTH NIGHT

Twelfth Night falls on the evening of the 5 January, when it is customary to take down all the Christmas decorations. Not to do so is considered bad luck because traditionally families decorated their houses with holly, ivy and mistletoe not only to make everything look pretty but also to give a warm, safe haven to the wood sprites through the most harsh time of the year. However, if one did not banish the wood sprites from the home, along with all the dying or dead foliage, after the twelve days were up the sprites would, legend has it, begin to cause mischief!

EPIPHANY

Epiphany or Three Kings' Day, as it is known in some countries, falls on 6 January. It marks the end of the twelve days of Christmas and celebrates the arrival of the Three Wise Men at the manger in Bethlehem. In translation, 'epiphany' means 'to reveal' or 'to show', which is precisely what the Wise Men did – that is, they revealed the presence of Jesus to the world. The colours of epiphany are normally white and gold, symbolizing newness and hope.

'Our children await Christmas presents like politicians getting election returns; there's the Uncle Fred precinct and the Aunt Ruth district still to come in.'

MARCELENE COX

'Perhaps the best Yuletide decoration is being wreathed in smiles.'

ANONYMOUS

ERIC AND ERNIE

Ernie: Christmas always brings out the best in people, doesn't it?

Eric: Well, you tell my wife that.

Ernie: Why, is she giving you trouble?

Eric: I'll say. She said to me today, 'You've done absolutely nothing to help with the Christmas dinner. Absolutely nothing.'

Ernie: What did you say to that?

Eric: I said, 'What! Look at the turkey. I bought it, I've plucked it and I've stuffed it!'

Ernie: Good for you!

Eric: Now, all *she's* got to do is kill it and put it in the oven.

FROM *THE MORECAMBE AND
WISE JOKE BOOK*, 1979

OH NO HE ISN'T!

Although pantomimes are occasionally performed in other countries, they are predominantly a British tradition that has gone from strength to strength down the centuries. The first pantomime is thought to have been performed in 1702 at the Drury Lane Theatre in central London. Composed by someone called Mr Weaver, the pantomime was called *The Tavern Bikers* and it was no doubt quite a dark piece, given that at that time panto was a mix of Italian *Commedia dell'Arte* and the French *Harliquinade*.

Nowadays, children and adults up and down the country enjoy pantomimes during the

season, which runs, roughly, from December to February. You are more likely to see celebrity guests and characters from your favourite soap opera performing rather than masked clowns. The most popular pantomimes follow traditional fairy tales such as *Cinderella*, *Puss in Boots*, *Aladdin*, *Babes in the Wood* and *Dick Wittington*.

AND GOOD CHEER TO NO ONE

Not everyone enjoys the Christmas period, as the following observation from British satirist and newspaper columnist, Victor Lewis-Smith shows: 'The most loathsome

of all this year's crass Yuletide innovations is surely the "ethical Christmas gift". Instead of a DVD or the handsome pair of socks you'd been hoping to receive, an ecologically crazed friend posts you a charity card informing you that "the money I would have spent on your present has been used to buy six chickens for an African farmer" or "a camel for a Bedouin tribesperson", and you're supposed to look pleased that he's given you precisely nothing, while he basks in a nauseating glow of self-satisfied eleemosynary.'

ONE TOO MANY

As well as being the season where everyone eats too much – alcohol is also often consumed to excess over the Christmas season. Take, for example, the time in 1863 when, having dined with Mark Twain at Barnum's restaurant in New York to celebrate Christmas, the author Artemis Ward stood up to make a speech. Or at least he tried to stand up but, finding himself unsuccessful, eventually slumped back down at the table declaring, 'Consider it standing'.

DECK THE HALLS

Deck the halls with boughs of holly,
fa la la la la la la la la!
'Tis the season to be jolly, fa la la la
la la la la la!
Don we now our gay apparel fa la
la la la la la la la!
Toll the ancient Yuletide carol, fa la
la la la la la la la!

See the blazing yule before us, fa la
la la la la la la la!
Strike the harp and join the chorus,
fa la la la la la la la!
Follow me in merry measure, fa la
la la la la la la la!
While I tell of Yuletide treasure, fa
la la la la la la la la!

*Fast away the old year passes, fa la
la la la la la la la!
Hail the new, ye lads and lasses, fa
la la la la la la la la!
Sing we joyous all together, fa la la
la la la la la la!
Heedless of the wind and weather,
fa la la la la la la la la!*

❧

'My first copies of Treasure Island
and Huckleberry Finn still have
some blue-spruce needles
scattered in the pages.
They smell of Christmas.'

CHARLTON HESTON

THE MASQUE OF CHRISTMAS

This play by Ben Jonson was first presented at court in 1616. It is said to contain the first recorded 'personification' of Father Christmas:

'He is attir'd in round Hose, long Stockings, a close Doublet, a high crown'd Hat with a Broach, a long thin beard, a Truncheon, little Ruffes, white Shoes, his Scarffes, and Garters tyed crosse, and his Drum beaten before him.'

> 'A good conscience is
> a continual Christmas.'
> BENJAMIN FRANKLIN

THE GLASTONBURY
THORN

The legend goes that soon
after Christ's death, Joseph of
Arimathea travelled to Britain
from the Holy Land to spread the
message of Christianity. Exhausted
after his long journey, it is said that
he lay down to rest and pushed his
staff into the ground beside him.
When he awoke he found that the

staff had taken root and began to grow and blossom. He left it there and it has flowered every spring and Christmas.

Although the original thorn eventually died, many cuttings had been taken, and it is said that one of these cuttings is still found in the grounds of Glastonbury Abbey today.

BIBLIOGRAPHY

Dearmer, Percy, Vaughn Williams, R, Shaw, Martin, *The Oxford Book of Carols*, Oxford University Press, 1972

Opie, Iona and Peter, *The Oxford Nursery Rhyme Book*, Oxford University Press, 1973

Jarski, Rosemarie, *Grumpy Old Wit*, Ebury Press, 2007

WEBSITES

www.christmas-time.com

www.woodlands-junior.kent.sch.uk

www.anecdotage.com

www.dgillan.screaming.net